The Perfect Client

Henry Allen

Copyright Page

Copyright Holder: © Henry Allen
Author: © Henry Allen 2025
Publisher: Univon

Release Year 2025

Index

What is a Perfect Client?

A perfect client is much more than someone who buys what you offer. They are a strategic ally of your business, a person or entity that not only meets your expectations, but also contributes to the growth and stability of your company. This client does not arise by chance; they are the result of identifying, understanding and attracting those who share values, needs and objectives aligned with those of your business. But how is it precisely defined? The answer begins with the most basic: the perfect client is someone who is easy, profitable and rewarding to work with, both for them and for you.

Imagine a customer who understands the value of your product or service from the first moment, who appreciates the effort behind what you offer and is willing to pay the right price for it. It's not just about selling, but about creating a relationship that benefits both parties. This type of customer respects the agreed terms, fulfills their commitments and provides value beyond the economic transaction. They can recommend you to others, help you improve with their feedback and, most importantly, become a natural advocate for your brand.

The perfect client, however, is not someone who simply says "yes" to everything. They are someone who challenges you constructively, who forces you to raise your standards because they value quality and seek the best. They are someone who trusts you and, at the same time, demands clear, measurable results. This doesn't mean they are unnecessarily demanding, but rather their level of expectation is a reflection of their appreciation for what you do.

A key aspect of the perfect customer is that their profile can vary depending on your type of business. For a software company, for example, the perfect customer may be an organization that understands the importance of technology and is committed to implementing long-term solutions. For a restaurant, it may be a person who values a complete dining experience, from the ambiance to the quality of the ingredients. In both cases, the important thing is that there is a fit between what your company offers and what the customer needs.

Knowing the perfect customer also means understanding their motivations. It's not just about what they buy, but why they buy it. Maybe they're looking to solve a specific problem, improve their quality of life, or achieve a particular goal. Identifying these motivations allows you to personalize your offering and ultimately strengthen your relationship with them. A perfect customer doesn't feel like just another number; they feel valued and understood, and that feeling translates into loyalty.

It's essential to recognize that not every client is perfect, and that's okay. Sometimes, attracting clients who aren't a good fit can be more costly in terms of time, resources, and energy. These clients, while well-intentioned, may require more attention than you can sustainably provide. So part of identifying your perfect client includes accepting that saying no to certain clients is also a way to protect the quality and stability of your business.

The perfect client is not an abstract idea, but a practical and achievable figure. It is someone who aligns with your company's values, who shares your expectations and who values what you do. It is a mutually beneficial relationship where both parties thrive. Building your business around this type of client is not only possible, but necessary if you want to have healthy sales and sustainable growth. It is not about attracting everyone, but about attracting those who really matter. These are the clients who transform a transaction into a shared success story.

Getting to Know Your Ideal Client

Knowing your ideal client is like finding the treasure map that leads you straight to success. If you don't know who they are, everything you do will be full of assumptions and random moves. But once you identify them, every decision becomes clearer, more precise and, above all, more effective. Knowing your ideal client is not just about knowing their name, age or where they live. It goes much deeper. It's about understanding what motivates them, what inspires them, what frustrates them and what makes them happy. When you manage to connect with that essence, everything changes.

The first step to knowing your ideal customer is to observe and listen. Ask yourself who is currently buying your products or services. Don't just focus on numbers, but on patterns. What do these people have in common? Why do they choose you over your competition? These questions are critical because they help you build a real profile based on data and not assumptions. For example, if you run a sportswear business, you might notice that most of your customers are active people between 25 and 40 years old who value quality and are looking to improve their physical performance. That information is not only useful, it's pure gold.

However, it is not enough to just look at those who already buy from you. You also need to identify people who are not yet your customers, but could be. This is where research comes in. Talk to your prospects, conduct surveys, analyze market trends. What are they looking for? What problems do they have that you can solve? At this point, technological tools such as social media, Google Analytics or CRMs are your best allies. These platforms provide you with data on interests, behaviors and preferences, helping you to increasingly refine the profile of your ideal customer.

The next step is to put yourself in their shoes. Ask yourself how your ideal customer lives. What do they do during the day? What kind of decisions do they make? What influences those decisions? For example, if your ideal customer is an entrepreneur, they likely value their time more than anything else. So how can you make your product or service save them time or make their life easier? This exercise in empathy not only helps you connect with them, but also tailor your offer to make it irresistible.

Knowing your ideal customer also means understanding their emotions. Purchasing decisions are rarely completely rational. People buy based on how something makes them feel. An ideal customer may choose your brand not just because of the quality of what you offer, but because they feel valued, understood, and connected to you. Think about the brands you choose. Why do you do that? Maybe it's because they offer you something beyond the product: trust, inspiration, or even a sense of belonging. That's what you need to replicate to attract your ideal customer.

One crucial aspect that many companies overlook is that ideal customers evolve. What they need today may not be the same as what they need tomorrow. That's why getting to know your ideal customer isn't a one-time exercise. It's an ongoing process. You need to be in constant communication with them, adjusting your offering and adapting to their changes. Stay alert to trends and how they affect your customers. If you can anticipate their needs, you'll not only be relevant, but indispensable.

Finally, knowing your ideal customer also means knowing when they aren't your customer. Not everyone will fit into your business, and that's okay. Don't try to be everything to everyone. If you try to please everyone, you'll probably please no one. Clearly define who your ideal customer is and focus on them. This will allow you to use your resources more efficiently and build stronger, longer-lasting relationships.

Knowing your ideal client is not a luxury, it is a necessity. It is the foundation on which a successful business is built. When you know who your client is, you know where to find them, how to talk to them, and how to offer them exactly what they need. You not only make your job easier, you also create a real impact on people's lives. And that, at the end of the day, is what defines a company that transcends.

Smart Segmentation

Smart segmentation is the process of dividing your market into specific, manageable groups based on common characteristics. It's like putting together a puzzle: Instead of trying to fit all the pieces together at once, you work on small sections that, when put together, form a complete picture. If you try to sell your product or service to everyone, you end up diluting your efforts and wasting resources. Segmentation allows you to focus your energy on those who are actually most likely to benefit from what you offer.

The first step to effective segmentation is to identify key criteria for dividing your market. These criteria can vary depending on the type of business you have. Generally speaking, the most common factors include demographics, geography, behaviors, and specific needs. For example, if you sell clothing, you might segment based on age, gender, or lifestyle. If you're a software company, you might want to divide your market based on the size of the companies you sell to or the industry they're in. The key is to choose criteria that really help you understand your customers better.

Segmentation is not a random process. You can't just divide your market based on vague ideas. You need concrete data. This means researching and collecting relevant information. Today, digital tools make this task easier. Google Analytics, social media, online surveys and market research are great allies. These tools allow you to analyse behaviour patterns, interests and preferences of your current and potential customers. Remember that the more specific you are when defining your segments, the more effective your approach will be.

Once you've defined your segments, it's important to evaluate them to make sure they're useful and viable. A good segment should be measurable, accessible, substantial, and differentiated. For example, if you create a segment that's too small, it may not be profitable to focus on it. On the other hand, if the segment is too broad, you may lose the precision you need to meet the specific needs of that group. Find the balance between detail and viability.

Segmentation doesn't end with the initial market split. It's also critical to customize your messages and strategies for each segment. Let's say you have two main segments: young people between 18 and 25 years old who are looking for innovative products and parents between 35 and 50 years old who prioritize safety and savings. The message for the first group should be exciting, dynamic and focused on technology or innovative design. In contrast, the message for parents should focus on reliability, practicality and economic benefits. Segmentation allows you to speak directly to each group in their own language.

In addition to tailoring your messaging, you also need to adjust your distribution strategy and communication channels. Each segment has its own path to reach you. Young people may be more receptive to ads on Instagram or TikTok, while parents may prefer receiving recommendations via email or social media like Facebook. The key is to be present where they are and offer them an experience that is comfortable and accessible to them.

An important aspect of smart segmentation is that it allows you to identify market opportunities that might go unnoticed if you focus on the general market. By analyzing different segments, you might notice unmet needs or areas where there is less competition. This can open doors for you to launch new products or services designed specifically for those niches. Segmentation not only optimizes your current efforts, but also inspires innovation and growth.

Segmentation is also a powerful tool for customer loyalty. By knowing your segments better, you can offer them more personalized and relevant treatment. For example, you can send exclusive promotions that align with a specific segment's interests or design loyalty programs that reflect their priorities. When customers feel that you understand them, they are more likely to stay with you for the long term.

Finally, remember that segmentation is not a static process. The market changes, customers evolve, and your strategies need to adapt. That's why it's important to regularly review and update your segments.

This will allow you to stay relevant and continue to meet your customers' needs effectively. Smart segmentation is not just a marketing tool; it's a comprehensive strategy for building meaningful relationships with your customers and maximizing the impact of your business.

The Signs of the Ideal Client

Recognizing an ideal client is like identifying the key pieces of a puzzle. While not every client comes with a sign that says, "I'm perfect for your business," there are clear signs that can help you spot them. These signs are like clues that, if interpreted correctly, will lead you to successful, long-lasting business relationships. But to pick up on these signs, you first need to know what to look for.

One of the first signs of an ideal client is their clarity about their needs. A client who knows exactly what they want or at least has a clear idea of what they need is much easier to serve. This type of client saves you time because it doesn't require lengthy discovery processes or constant adjustments to the solution you offer. For example, if you sell graphic design services and the client tells you they need a clean, modern logo with a specific color scheme, you already have a solid starting point. Their clarity allows you to work more efficiently and deliver something they truly value.

Another important sign is the customer's willingness to invest in what you offer. An ideal customer understands the value of your product or service and is willing to pay for it. They don't try to haggle over every detail or continually shop around for the lowest price. This doesn't mean they don't value a good deal, but they understand that quality comes at a price. This type of customer sees your offering as an investment rather than an expense, which makes the business relationship much easier. They are also less likely to create conflict over financial issues, which creates a smoother, more positive environment for both parties.

Effective communication is also a great sign of an ideal client. This client responds to your messages, is engaged in the process, and is willing to share relevant information to keep the work flowing smoothly. If you're working on a project and the client responds in a timely manner, provides constructive feedback, and shows interest in the progress, you're dealing with someone who values your time as much as their own. This level of communication makes any collaboration easier and more productive.

Respect for your expertise is another characteristic you can't overlook. An ideal client trusts you as an expert in what you do. They don't try to dictate how to do your job or belittle your recommendations. For example, if you're a consultant and the client accepts your strategies without unnecessarily questioning them, it shows that they respect your knowledge and trust your abilities. This creates an environment of mutual trust, which is essential for the success of any business relationship.

A less obvious, but equally important, sign is the customer's attitude toward long-term relationships. The ideal customer isn't thinking solely about the current transaction, but about how they can build a lasting relationship with you. They ask about other services you offer, show interest in working with you again, and recommend you to others. This type of customer understands that a good business relationship benefits both parties and is willing to make the commitment to make it work.

Another key indicator is the client's ability to adapt and be flexible. Business, like life, is full of unexpected events. An ideal client understands this and doesn't panic in the face of change. If something doesn't go exactly as expected, this client is willing to work out solutions with you rather than blaming you or giving up right away. Their positive, proactive attitude can make a huge difference, especially on complex or long-term projects.

Finally, the ideal client is also distinguished by being someone who aligns with your business values. If your company promotes sustainability, for example, and you find a client who shares that concern for the environment, you already have a deep connection that can strengthen the relationship. Shared values build trust and loyalty, and make work much more satisfying.

Identifying the signs of your ideal client isn't a one-time exercise. It's a process that requires practice, observation, and sometimes learning through experience. As you interact with more clients, you become more adept at recognizing these signs and acting accordingly. Remember that not every client will display all the signs right away, but the clearer and more consistent the indicators are, the more likely that relationship will be a success. Paying attention to these signs not only saves you trouble, it also brings you closer to the perfect client for your business.

The Art of Saying No

Saying no is one of the most important skills you can develop as an entrepreneur or professional, and, paradoxically, it is also one of the most difficult to master. In a world where the mantra of many businesses is to please the customer at all costs, turning down an opportunity or a project can seem risky, even unthinkable. However, learning to say no at the right time is a way to protect your time, your resources, and, above all, the quality of your work. It's not about being confrontational or rude, but about setting clear boundaries that benefit both your business and your ideal clients.

The first step in learning to say no is to recognize that not every client is a good fit for your business. While it can be tempting to take every opportunity that comes along, especially in the early stages of a startup, doing so can backfire. Taking on a client who doesn't align with your values, capabilities, or goals can create more trouble than it's worth. A difficult client can consume your time, wear down your team, and, in the worst case, damage your business's reputation. Saying no in these cases isn't a missed opportunity, it's a missed opportunity.

It's important to be clear about your criteria for accepting or rejecting a client or project. These criteria may include the available budget, the time needed to complete the work, the client's attitude, or even the nature of the project. For example, if a client insists on an unreasonably low price or impossible deadlines, it's a sign that the relationship won't be beneficial to either party. Knowing exactly what your boundaries are gives you the confidence to say no without hesitation.

When it comes time to turn down a client or project, how you do it is crucial. Saying no doesn't have to be rude or create conflict. In fact, the key is to be honest, professional, and direct, but always with empathy. For example, instead of saying, "I don't want to work with you," you could explain, "I don't think this project is right for us right now, but I really appreciate you considering us." This approach not only preserves the relationship, but it also demonstrates respect for the other person.

In some cases, saying no can even strengthen your reputation. Customers respect companies that know what they want and have the courage to stick to their principles. This positions you as a serious, trustworthy professional, someone who values quality over quantity. On the other hand, accepting everything that comes along can make you perceived as desperate or willing to compromise your standards, which can erode your credibility in the long run.

Another important aspect of saying no is understanding that it doesn't always mean an outright rejection. In many cases, you can offer mutually beneficial alternatives. For example, if a client asks for something that's outside your area of expertise, you might recommend another provider who can meet their needs. Not only does this help you keep your focus on what you do best, it also builds goodwill with the client and strengthens your professional network.

Saying no also involves internal discipline. Often, the temptation to accept everything comes from a fear of rejection or losing income. But accepting projects or clients that aren't a good fit can have a cost far greater than the initial benefit. Learning to prioritize and focus on the right opportunities is essential to the sustainable growth of your business. Every time you say no to something that doesn't fit, you're saying yes to something better: time for your ideal clients, energy for quality projects, and space for opportunities that really matter.

Finally, remember that saying no is a sign of respect for yourself and your team. Valuing your time and resources is just as important as valuing your customers. By setting clear boundaries and sticking to them, you send a powerful message: your business has a mission, standards, and a clear focus. And those are the foundations of any successful company.

Learning the art of saying no doesn't happen overnight. It's a process that takes practice, confidence, and sometimes even mistakes. But once you master it, you realize that it's not a negative word, but a powerful tool to create a stronger, more focused, and more rewarding business. Saying no doesn't close doors, it opens the right ones.

Evaluation Criteria

Having clear criteria for evaluating your potential clients is essential to making smart, strategic decisions in your business. It's not about judging or discriminating, but rather about making sure that the business relationship is mutually beneficial. By establishing these criteria, you're building a filter that helps you identify the clients who really add value to your company and avoid those who could become a burden.

The first criterion you should consider is the alignment between the client's needs and the solutions you offer. Before you engage with a client, ask yourself if you can actually solve their problem or meet their need effectively. Taking on projects that are not within your area of expertise or that require resources you don't have can lead to mediocre results and frustration for both parties. Evaluate whether your products or services are designed to specifically address what the client needs. If not, it's best to be honest from the start and, if possible, refer the client to someone who can better help them.

Another important criterion is budget. An ideal client understands and respects the value of your work, which is reflected in their willingness to pay a fair price. Assess whether the client has a realistic budget and is willing to invest in the quality you offer. It's important to be clear about your pricing and terms from the start to avoid misunderstandings or long-winded negotiations. If a client insists on lowering the price or getting additional services at no cost, this may be a sign that they don't fully value your work.

Communication is also a key factor. A client who communicates clearly, honestly, and openly makes any project much easier. Evaluate how the client behaves during the first interactions. Does he or she respond to your messages in a timely manner? Does he or she explain his or her needs in detail? Does he or she listen to your recommendations? The quality of the initial communication is a good indicator of how the relationship will be in the long term. If a client is difficult to reach, inconsistent, or unclear from the beginning, these difficulties are likely to persist.

Another criterion to consider is the client's attitude toward collaboration. An ideal client not only seeks results, but is also willing to work with you to achieve them. This includes being open to suggestions, providing constructive feedback, and holding up their end of the bargain, such as delivering information or meeting deadlines. Assess whether the client seems interested in building a team relationship or whether, on the contrary, they seem to expect you to do everything without their input. Collaboration is key to the success of any project.

The client's history is another aspect to consider. If they are a repeat client, evaluate what your previous experiences with them have been like. Does they keep their commitments? Does they respect deadlines and contract terms? If they are a new client, do some research on their reputation. This is especially important if you work in an industry where references and connections are essential. A client with a problematic history, such as late payments or constant changes in agreed terms, may not be the best option, no matter how attractive the project may seem.

Long-term projection should also be part of your evaluation criteria. Ask yourself if this client has the potential to become a repeat client or if the relationship will likely be a one-time thing. Clients who see value in your services and are willing to work with you long-term are often more valuable than those who are just looking for a quick, cheap fix. This doesn't mean you should automatically rule out one-time projects, but it's important to consider how they fit into your overall business goals.

A less obvious but equally important criterion is compatibility with your company's values. Assess whether the client shares or respects the principles that guide your business. For example, if your company has a strong commitment to sustainability, working with a client who doesn't value environmental impact could create tensions. Value alignment not only makes the relationship easier, it also makes the work more satisfying and meaningful.

Finally, intuition also plays a big role. Sometimes, after analyzing all the criteria above, something may just not feel right.

Maybe the client seems too demanding, or perhaps there are subtle signs that it won't be an easy relationship. Trust your gut. If something doesn't seem to fit, it's best to investigate further or even turn down the opportunity before you commit and face bigger problems later on.

Defining and applying evaluation criteria not only improves the quality of your business relationships, but also saves you time, energy and resources. It is an exercise that requires honesty and discipline, but in the long term it will allow you to build a solid base of ideal clients that contribute to the growth and stability of your business. Evaluate carefully, decide with confidence and build relationships that are truly worthwhile.

The Psychology of the Perfect Client

Understanding the psychology of the perfect customer is like having a map that guides you through the complexities of business relationships. It's not just about knowing what a customer needs, but understanding why they need it, what motivates them, and how they make decisions. This understanding not only improves the way you communicate with your customers, but also helps you build deeper, more meaningful relationships based on trust and mutual value.

The first key aspect of perfect customer psychology is motivation. Every customer has a reason behind their purchasing decisions. It could be to solve a problem, improve something in their life or business, save time, or even fulfill an emotional need, such as feeling more confident or successful. Your job is to identify that core motivation. Ask yourself, what does this customer really want? For example, if you sell business management systems, your customer might be motivated by a desire to reduce errors, improve efficiency, or stand out from the competition. When you understand this motivation, you can adjust your approach and message to connect directly with what matters to the customer.

Another key aspect is the perception of value. Customers don't buy products or services, they buy the benefit they think they will get from them. The perfect customer is one who clearly perceives the value of what you offer and connects it with their own needs. That's why it's crucial to communicate not only the features of your product or service, but also the results it generates. For example, if you offer financial advice, don't just describe the tools you use. Instead, show how these tools can help the customer achieve their financial goals and feel more comfortable about their financial future.

Trust plays a huge role in the psychology of the perfect client. Most people are naturally cautious, especially when it comes to spending money or committing to something new. A perfect client trusts you because they perceive that you are an expert in your field and genuinely interested in helping them. Building this trust starts with transparency. Be clear about what you offer, what you don't offer, and what the client can expect from working with you. Keep your promises, even the small ones, because every interaction either reinforces or weakens the client's perception of you.

Customer purchasing behavior is also influenced by their emotions. Even seemingly logical decisions often have an underlying emotional component. For example, a customer may purchase a business software because it will help them automate processes, but the emotion behind that decision may be the relief of reducing their stress or the satisfaction of having more time to pursue their passions. Recognizing and responding to these emotions gives you an edge in how you present your proposition. Talk not only about the practical benefits, but also about the positive emotional impact your product or service can have.

Another key psychological element is the desire to feel understood. Perfect customers value vendors who take the time to listen to them, understand their problems, and offer customized solutions. To achieve this, practice active empathy. Listen to what your customers say, but also pay attention to what they don't say. For example, if a customer mentions that they're looking to cut costs, they might be expressing a deeper concern for the financial stability of their business. Responding to these concerns proactively shows that you care about more than just the transaction.

Reciprocity is also a powerful psychological principle. Perfect clients are often more inclined to work with you when they perceive that you have done something valuable for them first. This can be as simple as offering a free consultation, sharing helpful information, or showing genuine interest in their goals. This initial act of generosity creates a positive bond and increases the likelihood that the client will decide to continue the relationship.

Additionally, the need to belong influences how customers engage with brands. Many people want to feel part of something bigger, whether it's a community, a movement, or a mission. Perfect customers don't just choose your products or services because they serve a purpose, but because they resonate with what your company stands for. By clearly communicating your business values and how they are reflected in your products, you'll attract customers who not only want to buy, but also support what you do.

Finally, there's the issue of engagement. Perfect customers don't just make a purchase and walk away. They want to invest in a long-term relationship because they trust that they'll continue to get value from it. To foster this type of engagement, make it easy for customers to come back to you. Offer incentives for future purchases, maintain consistent communication, and most importantly, keep delivering value in every interaction. A customer who feels valued and cared for is more likely to remain loyal and recommend you to others.

Understanding the psychology of the perfect customer isn't something you achieve overnight. It requires observation, practice, and a constant effort to put yourself in the customer's shoes. But once you start thinking like them, you can anticipate their needs, respond to their concerns, and ultimately build relationships that are not only profitable, but also fulfilling and long-lasting. The key is to always remember that behind every customer is a person with unique motivations, emotions, and expectations. Connecting with those human dimensions is what turns an ordinary business into an exceptional one.

Educate the Customer

Educating your customer is one of the most valuable strategies you can implement to build strong and productive relationships with your customers. Many people believe that selling means only offering a product or service, but the reality is that the customer needs to understand what they are buying, how it works, and how they can benefit from it. An educated customer not only makes more informed decisions, but also has more confidence in their purchase and, most importantly, in you as a provider.

The first step in educating your customers is to recognize that not everyone has the same level of knowledge about your industry, your product, or the problem they're trying to solve. Many customers may not be familiar with technical terms, available tools, or even the options available to them. Therefore, it's your responsibility to tailor your communication to be accessible and easy to understand. Use clear, direct language, avoid unnecessary jargon, and focus on explaining things from the customer's perspective, not yours as an expert.

An effective way to educate customers is to anticipate their questions. Ask yourself, what does a customer need to know to make an informed decision? For example, if you sell a digital marketing service, your customers may wonder what makes your strategies different from other vendors, how you will measure results, and how long it will take to see improvements. If you provide clear, detailed answers to these questions before they even ask them, you will be demonstrating your expertise and building trust from the start.

Educational materials are a key tool in this process. They can include guides, articles, videos, infographics, case studies, and even webinars. These resources not only serve to teach customers about your products or services, but also to position you as a reference in your field. For example, if you own a technology store, you can create videos that explain how to install and use the devices you sell. Not only does this help the customer feel more confident in their purchase, but it also reinforces the perception that you really care about their experience.

Another important part of educating your customer is helping them understand the value of what you offer. Often times, customers may be hesitant about pricing or the benefits of your product because they don't fully understand what they're getting. This is where education plays a crucial role. Don't just mention features, explain how those features solve specific problems or improve the customer's life. For example, if you offer management software, don't just talk about its features; describe how those features can save time, reduce errors, and improve productivity.

It's important to note that educating doesn't mean imposing. Some customers may not be ready to absorb all the information at once, and that's okay. Your job is to provide them with the necessary knowledge at the right time, so that they don't feel overwhelmed. For example, if a customer shows interest in a product but doesn't seem convinced, you can offer a demo or a free consultation to clear up their doubts and help them visualize how your solution can benefit them.

Patience is essential when it comes to educating customers. Not everyone will learn at the same pace or have the same level of initial interest. However, if you take the time to answer questions, guide processes, and provide relevant information, you will be building a solid foundation of trust and loyalty. Customers remember and value companies that care about their success and not just about closing a sale.

Educating also means managing expectations. This means being honest about what your product or service can and cannot do. It's tempting to promise spectacular results to close a sale, but this only leads to dissatisfaction if the customer's expectations are not met. Instead, explain clearly what they can expect and what actions they can take to maximize results. For example, if you offer a fitness plan, make it clear that the results will depend on the customer's effort and consistency, as well as the resources you provide.

An additional aspect of educating customers is teaching them to make informed decisions. This doesn't mean manipulating them, but rather empowering them to choose what they really need. You can do this by providing them with comparisons between options, explaining the pros and cons of each, and guiding them to evaluate which one best suits their circumstances. A customer who feels like they had control over their decision will be more likely to trust you and be satisfied with their choice.

Finally, remember that customer education is not a one-time effort, but rather an ongoing process. Even after the customer has purchased your product or service, it is still important to offer support and knowledge. This can include additional training, updates on new features, or simply being available to answer questions. By keeping this communication open, you will be fostering a long-term relationship that can translate into repeat business, referrals, and increased loyalty.

Educating your customer doesn't just benefit the customer, it benefits your business as well. A well-informed customer is less likely to create conflict, more likely to become a repeat customer, and more inclined to recommend your services to others. Putting time and effort into this task may seem like a considerable investment, but the results are well worth it. You're building a solid foundation for long-term growth and success, both for your customers and for yourself.

Effective Communication

Effective communication is the backbone of any successful business relationship. No matter how good your product or service is, if you don't know how to communicate clearly and efficiently with your customers, you will miss opportunities and leave a smaller impact than you could have. The key to effective communication is to convey your ideas in a way that is understood, valued and remembered by your customer, while also making sure you fully understand their needs and expectations.

The first step to effective communication is listening. While this may sound simple, it actually takes practice and attention. Listening isn't just about waiting for the other person to finish speaking before responding. It's about being present, taking in not only what the customer is saying, but also how they are saying it. Pay attention to their tone of voice, their facial expressions, and the words they use. These details can give you important clues about what they really need and how they feel about the conversation. By showing genuine interest and asking relevant questions, you'll be laying a solid foundation for a trusting relationship.

Another crucial aspect of effective communication is clarity. Misunderstandings often occur when information is not presented in a clear and organized manner. Make sure your message is easy to understand. Avoid using technical language or complex terms that may confuse the customer, unless you are sure they understand them. For example, if you are explaining how a service works, break it down into simple steps and use concrete examples to illustrate your point. Clear communication not only prevents confusion, but also shows that you respect the customer's time and attention.

Empathy is an essential ingredient in effective communication. Putting yourself in the customer’s shoes helps you adjust your message to better resonate with their concerns and priorities. For example, if a customer is concerned about the cost of a service, instead of simply defending your price, explain how your solution can offer value and save them money in the long run.

Empathy not only improves the quality of your interactions, but it also allows you to build more human and authentic relationships.

Adapting your communication style to the customer's preferences is another important aspect. Some people prefer direct and quick communications, while others need more details and explanations. Identifying this style can make a big difference. If a customer seems to be the type who values brevity, avoid overloading them with too much information. Conversely, if someone seems to want to understand every detail, take the time to dig deeper and answer all their questions. This adaptation shows that you are attentive to their needs and preferences.

Consistency also plays a big role in effective communication. Customers appreciate it when they know what to expect from you. If you promise something, deliver. If you say you'll respond within a certain time frame, make sure you do. Being consistent in your words and actions creates a sense of reliability that strengthens your customer relationship. Even when problems or unforeseen events arise, maintaining honest and transparent communication can help you maintain customer trust.

In addition to being clear and consistent, it's important to be proactive in your communication. Don't wait for the client to contact you with questions or concerns. Get ahead of the game and provide relevant information before it's needed. For example, if you're working on a project with a client, send them regular updates on progress. Not only does this demonstrate professionalism, it also reduces the client's anxiety knowing everything is under control.

Another essential point is positive language. The words you use can influence how the customer feels about the interaction. Even when you have to deliver bad news or handle a complaint, try to frame your message in a positive way. Instead of saying something isn’t possible, offer alternatives. For example, if a customer requests a service that you can’t provide, instead of simply saying no, you could respond with something like: we don’t offer that right now, but what I can recommend is this other option that might work really well for you. This approach not only diffuses the situation, but it also shows your willingness to help.

Feedback is another valuable element in effective communication. Don't be afraid to ask your customers what they think about your service or how you can improve. Listening to their opinions not only gives you useful information, but it also shows them that you value their perspective. Plus, when you act on that feedback, you're strengthening the relationship and showing that you really care about what they have to say.

Finally, remember that effective communication doesn't end after the sale or deal is closed. Keep in touch with your customers, even after they've used your product or service. This can be as simple as sending a message to make sure they're satisfied or sharing helpful information that might interest them. This ongoing communication not only helps build loyalty, but it also keeps you top of mind for future opportunities.

Effective communication is both an art and a science. It requires patience, practice, and a willingness to learn and adapt to each client. But the benefits are huge. By improving your communication skills, you not only strengthen your relationships with clients, but you also increase the chances of long-term success for your business. The key is to remember that every interaction is an opportunity to build trust, solve problems, and create value—and that strong communication is the bridge that connects all of these things.

The Client as Ambassador

Turning your customers into brand ambassadors is one of the most powerful strategies you can implement to expand your business. A satisfied customer who speaks positively about your company to their friends, family, and colleagues carries much more weight than any advertising campaign. Personal recommendations build trust, and that trust translates into new opportunities. But how do you get your customers to become ambassadors? It's not a matter of luck, but of building authentic relationships, providing exceptional experiences, and fostering an emotional connection with your brand.

The first step in turning a customer into an ambassador is to make sure they are completely satisfied with your product or service. This starts from the first contact they have with you. Make sure their experience is flawless, from the clarity of your communication to the quality of what you offer. If a customer has an outstanding experience, they will be much more likely to rave about you. For example, if you run a restaurant, it is not enough that the food is delicious; the service must be excellent, the atmosphere welcoming, and every detail taken care of. A memorable experience is what drives people to share their enthusiasm with others.

The key to creating ambassadors is to create an emotional connection. Customers don't just want to buy a product or service, they want to feel connected to something bigger. This can be your company's purpose, your values, or even your personal story as an entrepreneur. Share your mission authentically. If your company supports social causes, is eco-friendly, or has a human focus, make sure customers know that. A customer who identifies with your values will not only buy what you offer, but will want to share it with others because they feel like by doing so, they are also contributing to something meaningful.

Another way to motivate your customers to become ambassadors is to make them feel valued and special. We all like to be recognized, and your customers are no exception. A simple gesture, such as a personalized thank you message, can make a difference. If you have the opportunity, celebrate with them their achievements, special dates, or milestones related to your product. For example, if you run a gym, you could congratulate a customer for reaching a fitness goal. These details build a relationship of trust and affection, which increases the likelihood that they will recommend you.

Social media is a powerful tool to amplify the voice of your ambassadors. Create opportunities for your customers to share their experiences organically. For example, you could run contests, ask them to post photos using your products, or invite them to leave online reviews. Make sure to publicly thank them for their contributions and, if possible, offer them incentives. It doesn't have to be expensive; a small discount, a gift, or even public recognition can be enough to show them that you value their support.

It's important to remember that an ambassador doesn't just come out of nowhere. Often, customers need a little nudge to become active promoters of your brand. This can be achieved through referral programs, where you reward customers who bring in new business. However, the approach should be genuine and not feel like a cold transaction. The goal is to motivate already satisfied customers to talk about you more, not pressure them into doing so out of obligation. If the customer feels like they're being rewarded for something they would do anyway, the referral will be authentic and much more effective.

It's also critical to provide after-sales service that reinforces the customer experience. Many businesses miss opportunities to create ambassadors because they neglect the customer after the sale. Keep in touch, make sure they're enjoying your product or service, and resolve any issues quickly. If a customer feels like you're there to support them even after they've paid, they'll become a loyal advocate for your brand.

A customer ambassador is someone who not only believes in what you do, but is willing to advocate for it in front of others. To achieve this, you must be consistent in the quality of your product, the service you provide, and the values you communicate.

It's also important to accept and handle criticism in a professional manner. Sometimes even dissatisfied customers can become ambassadors if they see that you take their feedback seriously and strive to improve.

Finally, recognize that not every customer will become an ambassador, and that's okay. Some people simply want to enjoy the product or service without getting involved beyond that. The important thing is to identify those who show a natural enthusiasm and give them the tools and motivation to share their experience. By focusing your efforts on these key customers, you'll be building a powerful network of advocates who will amplify your message and attract more people to your business.

Turning customers into ambassadors not only benefits your company, it also creates a community around your brand. These relationships aren't just transactions, they're human connections that have the power to transform your business. When you make a customer feel valued, heard, and part of something bigger, you're establishing a relationship that goes far beyond a simple purchase. That's the magic of ambassadors: they're not just satisfied customers, they're allies who want to see you succeed.

Retention as a Key Strategy

Customer retention is one of the most important and often underestimated strategies in business. While many companies focus their efforts on attracting new customers, keeping existing ones is not only more cost-effective, but also critical to building a strong, sustainable foundation. A customer who sticks with you over time not only generates recurring revenue, but can also become an advocate for your brand, recommending you to others and strengthening your reputation in the market.

The first step to achieving high retention is providing an exceptional experience from the start. This doesn't just mean meeting customer expectations, but exceeding them. When someone interacts with your business, they should feel like they're receiving something unique and valuable—something they couldn't easily find elsewhere. This can be achieved through impeccable customer service, personalized attention, or small touches that show you truly care about their satisfaction. For example, if you run a clothing business, offering special packaging or including a personalized note can make all the difference and leave a lasting impression.

A key aspect of retention is understanding that the relationship with a customer doesn't end when they make a purchase. This is where the real work begins. Maintaining contact is crucial. This doesn't mean bombarding the customer with emails or messages, but rather finding meaningful ways to stay on their radar. A newsletter offering relevant content, a follow-up call to make sure they're happy with their purchase, or even a message on special dates like their birthday are all effective ways to build a stronger connection. These small actions may seem simple, but they have a profound impact on the customer's perception of your business.

Another important factor is showing that you value customer loyalty. People want to feel that their preference for your business is recognized. Loyalty programs are a great tool for this purpose. Offering exclusive discounts, rewards for repeat purchases, or early access to new products are all ways to thank customers for sticking with you.

However, it's important that these benefits are genuine and meaningful. If a customer feels that you're rewarding them only symbolically, the effort can lose its effect.

Problem resolution is another key pillar in customer retention. No matter how well you run your business, problems will inevitably arise at some point. What really matters is how you respond to those challenges. A customer who experiences a problem but sees you resolve it quickly, honestly, and efficiently often ends up more satisfied than one who never had an issue. How you handle these difficult situations shows the character of your business and can be the difference between losing a customer or earning their loyalty forever.

Personalization also plays a crucial role in retention. Customers don’t want to feel like just another number; they want to be treated as unique individuals with specific needs. This means remembering their preferences, offering them products or services that genuinely interest them, and tailoring your interactions to make them feel valued. If you run an online business, for example, using past purchase data to suggest relevant products is a great way to show that you're paying attention.

Additionally, transparency and honesty are essential to maintaining customer trust. If something doesn't go as planned, whether it's a delivery delay or an order error, be clear and take responsibility. Customers appreciate when companies are upfront and willing to correct their mistakes. Trying to hide or downplay problems only breeds distrust and can seriously damage the relationship.

Another important aspect of retention is constant innovation. Customers want to feel like they are associated with a brand that is evolving and adapting to their needs. This doesn't mean you have to constantly reinvent your business, but it does mean keeping an eye on trends, listening to your customers' feedback, and continually improving your offering. For example, if you run a gym and notice that many of your customers are interested in virtual classes, considering offering this option can be a great way to keep them engaged.

Open communication is key to building long-lasting relationships with customers. Asking them directly what they think about your business, what they would like to improve, or what additional services they would be interested in not only gives you valuable information, but also shows them that you value their opinion. Surveys, casual conversations, and social media comments are all effective ways to gather this feedback. The most important thing is to act on what you learn. If a customer feels that their opinion truly influences how you run your business, they are much more likely to stay with you.

Last but not least, remember that retention is not a short-term goal. It is an ongoing commitment that requires time, effort, and dedication. It is not just about keeping current customers, but about creating such a positive experience that they become loyal advocates for your brand. Every interaction, no matter how small, is an opportunity to reinforce that relationship and build a customer base that will not only buy, but also recommend and promote your business.

Retention not only boosts your revenue steadily, but it also reduces the costs associated with acquiring new customers. It's a key strategy that allows your business to grow sustainably, create deep connections with your audience, and stand out in an increasingly competitive market. By focusing your efforts on nurturing the customers you already have, you'll be investing in the long-term stability and success of your company.

The Value of Long-Term Relationships

Building long-term relationships with customers is not only a smart strategy, it is the foundation of a solid and sustainable business. In a world where everything seems to revolve around immediacy, companies that focus on cultivating long-lasting relationships stand out for their ability to generate trust, loyalty and stability. A customer who stays with you over time is not only a recurring source of income, but also a strategic ally that can boost the growth of your business. However, achieving these types of relationships requires commitment, effort and, above all, a mindset focused on mutual value.

Long-term relationships start with trust. When a customer trusts your business, they are more willing to stick with you, even when issues arise or competitors try to lure them away with tempting offers. This trust is not earned overnight, but is built with consistency and honesty. Every interaction with your customer is an opportunity to demonstrate your integrity. Delivering on your promises, being transparent in your communications, and acting responsibly are key pillars to establishing a solid foundation in any business relationship.

The value of these relationships is that a loyal customer not only buys more, but is also willing to pay more. A customer who feels an emotional connection to your brand doesn't choose your product or service solely on price, but on the entire experience you offer. This type of customer isn't constantly looking for alternatives, which means you don't have to compete solely on cost, something that can be detrimental to the sustainability of your business. Plus, customer loyalty often translates into referrals to friends and family, amplifying your reach without the need to spend on advertising.

To foster long-term relationships, it's crucial to understand that every customer has unique needs and expectations. You can't treat everyone the same and expect positive results. Personalization is key. This means taking the time to learn about your customers, their preferences, and how they interact with your product or service. If you run a technology business, for example, you can offer personalized technical support to solve specific problems. If you run a cafe, you might remember your regular customers' typical order. These small actions may seem insignificant, but they have a huge impact on how the customer perceives your business.

Constant communication also plays a key role in building long-lasting relationships. Keeping in touch with your customers shows that you care about their experience beyond the initial purchase. This can be achieved through informative emails, surveys to gather feedback, or even follow-up calls to make sure everything is working as they expected. However, this communication needs to be authentic and relevant. It's not about inundating your customers with messages, but about providing value in every interaction.

Another important aspect of long-term relationships is being there for your customers at key moments. If you know their birthdays, anniversaries, or any relevant milestones, acknowledge those dates in a meaningful way. It doesn't have to be expensive; a personalized message, a small discount, or even a simple thank you can make a big difference. These actions show that you don't see your customers as numbers, but as people with whom you have a genuine connection.

It's important to remember that long-term relationships won't always be perfect. There will be times when challenges, misunderstandings, or mistakes arise. In these situations, your response is what will truly define the relationship. Customers don't expect you to be perfect, but they do expect you to take responsibility and act to correct problems. Offering sincere apologies, finding quick solutions, and showing that you're willing to improve can turn a negative experience into an opportunity to strengthen the relationship.

Additionally, it's essential to recognize that long-term relationships require a mutual commitment. It's not just about what the customer can do for your business, but also what you can do for them. Listen to their needs, anticipate their problems, and tailor your services to provide an experience that truly makes their lives easier. When customers feel that you are invested in their success, they are much more inclined to be loyal to your brand.

Another key benefit of these relationships is the stability they provide for your business. A loyal customer provides predictable revenue, which makes planning and growth easier. Instead of constantly spending resources on acquiring new customers, you can focus on improving the experience for the ones you already have, which often results in higher profit margins. Additionally, loyal customers tend to be more receptive to trying new products or services you offer, which opens up opportunities to diversify and expand your business more efficiently.

It's also important to note that long-term relationships create an emotional impact for both the customer and the business. A customer who feels valued becomes a natural advocate for your brand, while a business that builds meaningful relationships finds a purpose beyond profit. This type of human connection creates a company culture that benefits not only your customers, but also your team, who will feel motivated by seeing the positive impact of their work.

Ultimately, the value of long-term relationships lies in their ability to transform your business into more than just a transaction. When you build a community of loyal customers, you're creating an ecosystem where everyone benefits. Customers get the value and attention they seek, while you build a sustainable business that not only survives, but thrives. It's an approach that requires patience, dedication, and care, but the results are invaluable. Long-term relationships aren't just a strategy — they're the essence of a successful, human business.

Managing Expectations

Managing your customers' expectations is one of the most important skills you can develop as a business owner or entrepreneur. Not only does this practice help you avoid conflict, it also builds a strong relationship based on trust and transparency. When a customer's expectations are aligned with what your business can offer, it creates more harmonious, less tense, and ultimately longer-lasting relationships. However, if expectations are unrealistic or poorly managed, frustrations and disappointments can arise that negatively impact the perception of your brand.

The first step in managing expectations is to be clear from the start. This means communicating precisely what you offer, how you offer it, and what the limits of your services or products are. If you sell a product, make sure your descriptions are honest and detailed. If you offer a service, explain exactly what is included, how long it will take, and what results can be expected. Clarity in initial communication is key to avoiding misunderstandings later on. For example, if you promise to deliver a project in a week, but in reality it takes ten days, you are setting the stage for unnecessary disappointment.

Another key aspect is setting realistic expectations. We all want to impress our customers, but promising more than we can deliver is a recipe for disaster. Instead of trying to impress with grandiose promises, it's better to under-deliver and then exceed what the customer expects. For example, if you know you can deliver an order in five days, you could tell the customer it will be ready in seven days. If you deliver ahead of schedule, you've exceeded their expectations and created a positive experience. Not only does this approach reduce stress for you, it also creates a sense of surprise and satisfaction for the customer.

Managing expectations also involves constant communication throughout the process. Even when you've been clear from the start, it's important to keep the customer informed at every stage. If an unexpected delay arises, don't wait for the customer to contact you to ask what's going on. Take the initiative and let them know as soon as possible, explaining the situation and offering solutions. This type of proactive communication shows that you value the customer and are invested in their experience. Plus, it significantly reduces frustration, as the customer feels like they're aware of what's going on.

One area where many companies fail at managing expectations is problem resolution. Customers don't expect everything to be perfect, but they do expect you to act quickly and efficiently when something goes wrong. If a product has a defect or a service doesn't live up to its promise, the worst thing you can do is minimize the problem or ignore it. Instead, acknowledge the mistake, sincerely apologize, and work on a solution that is satisfactory to the customer. This approach not only solves the problem at hand, but also reinforces the customer's trust in your business.

Training your team also plays a big role in managing expectations. Every person who interacts with a customer should be aligned with your business's values and policies. This means everyone should be consistent in how they communicate what you can offer and how they handle requests or concerns. If one member of your team promises something you can't deliver, the customer won't blame that person—they'll blame your business as a whole. That's why it's essential that everyone is working from the same information and standards.

Another crucial aspect is managing long-term expectations. This is especially important in ongoing business relationships. For example, if you are working with a client on a multi-month project, it is important to have clear, defined milestones along the way. It is not enough to promise a spectacular end result; the client needs to see tangible progress to maintain confidence in the process. Providing regular updates and demonstrating consistent progress helps keep expectations at a reasonable and manageable level.

Furthermore, managing expectations doesn't just mean meeting them, but also educating your clients about what is possible and what isn't. In many cases, clients come to you with preconceived ideas that may not be realistic or practical. It’s your job as an expert to guide them to a clearer understanding of what they really need and how you can help them achieve it. This requires communication skills, patience, and empathy. By taking the time to explain why certain things aren’t feasible and offering alternatives that are, you’re not only managing their expectations, but you’re also building your credibility as a professional.

Finally, remember that expectation management is an ongoing process. It's not something you do once and forget about. Every interaction with a customer is an opportunity to reaffirm what they can expect from you and to adjust those expectations as needed. Even the most loyal customers need reminders from time to time about what your business can offer and how they can get the most out of your products or services.

When you manage expectations effectively, you not only avoid conflict and misunderstandings, but you also create an environment where customers feel valued and understood. This, in turn, fosters loyalty, generates referrals, and strengthens your business's reputation. Managing expectations isn't just a skill—it's an investment in positive relationships and the long-term success of your business.

Sustainable Growth

Sustainable growth is the foundation for building a business that not only thrives in the short term, but is also able to meet the challenges and opportunities of the future. While it is tempting to pursue rapid growth, this approach often proves unsustainable, leading to problems such as loss of quality, resource overload, or even bankruptcy. Sustainable growth, on the other hand, is about moving forward in a steady and balanced manner, ensuring that each step taken strengthens your company rather than weakens it.

The first step toward sustainable growth is understanding that not all opportunities are equal. Often, companies fall into the trap of accepting any client, project, or market that comes their way, without considering whether it truly fits with their vision, capabilities, and resources. This approach can generate quick revenue, but it can also lead to burnout of your team and a decrease in the quality of your products or services. To grow sustainably, you must be selective and prioritize those opportunities that are aligned with the long-term goals of your business.

A key aspect of sustainable growth is planning. This involves setting clear, realistic goals that you can achieve without compromising quality or customer experience. Short-term goals should be connected to your long-term objectives, creating a clear path to growth. For example, if you run a service business, you might set an initial goal of increasing your customer base by 10 percent this year, while focusing on building strong internal processes to handle that increase efficiently.

Your business's ability to handle growth also plays a crucial role. Before you look to expand, make sure your systems, processes, and staff are prepared to take on an increased workload. Growing too quickly without a solid foundation can lead to errors, delays, and a poor customer experience. For example, if you plan to increase production at your company, you need to make sure you have the necessary infrastructure in place — from equipment to trained staff — to handle that growth without compromising quality.

Proper management of financial resources is another pillar of sustainable growth. Many businesses fail because they try to expand faster than their finances allow. It is essential to maintain a balance between reinvesting in the business and maintaining a stable financial base. For example, if you make extra profits, instead of spending them all on new initiatives, you could allocate a portion of them to a reserve fund to cover unforeseen events. This will allow you to handle unexpected situations without putting the stability of your business at risk.

Your relationship with your customers is also a key determinant of sustainable growth. As you grow, it's crucial to maintain the same level of attention and care you offered when you had fewer customers. Loyal customers are a constant source of revenue and referrals, which can naturally boost your growth. If growth negatively impacts the quality of your products or customer experience, you risk losing their trust, which can be difficult to regain. Investing in tools and technologies that help you better manage your customer relationships can be an effective way to ensure that they don't feel neglected.

Another essential component is the ongoing development of your team. As your business grows, your employees must grow with it. This means investing in training, creating opportunities for professional development, and ensuring your team is aligned with your company's vision and values. A motivated and well-trained team is not only more productive, but also better able to handle the challenges that come with growth. Plus, an engaged team can be one of the best tools to boost your business, as they are directly involved in creating value for your customers.

Innovation is also an important driver of sustainable growth. You can't rely solely on what works today to ensure success tomorrow. Exploring new ideas, trying different approaches, and adapting to changes in the market are practices that will help you stay relevant. However, innovation must be balanced with the capacity of your business. Introducing too many changes at once can lead to confusion for both your team and your customers. Instead, take a gradual approach, implementing and testing new ideas in a controlled manner.

Sustainability also involves taking care of the impact your business has on its surroundings. This doesn't just refer to the environment – although reducing your ecological footprint is a valuable strategy – but also how your business affects the people and communities it interacts with. Make sure your business practices are ethical and responsible, and consider how you can positively contribute to the lives of your employees, customers, and society at large. A business that operates responsibly not only earns the trust of its customers, but also creates a solid foundation for long-term growth.

Finally, sustainable growth requires patience. In a world where everything seems to revolve around immediate results, it's easy to be tempted to look for quick fixes. However, building a solid business takes time. Every step you take, no matter how small, is an investment in your company's future. Celebrate achievements, learn from challenges, and stay focused on the bigger picture.

Sustainable growth is not about growing at any cost, but about growing in ways that strengthen your business, benefit your customers, and create lasting value. By taking a balanced, strategic, and responsible approach, you will not only ensure your business's success today, but also prepare it to face the future with confidence and resilience. Growing sustainably is a conscious decision that can make the difference between fleeting success and a lasting legacy.

Adaptation to New Markets

Adapting to new markets is one of the most exciting and challenging strategies a business can undertake. Expanding into uncharted territory or diversifying your offering to serve a different audience means stepping outside your comfort zone, but it also opens the door to significant growth opportunities. However, this transition is not easy and requires planning, research, and above all, flexibility. The key to successfully adapting to new markets is to thoroughly understand their unique characteristics and adjust your business to meet the specific needs of that environment.

The first step in this process is research. You can't enter a new market without understanding who you're going to serve, what their preferences are, and how your products or services fit into their lifestyle. This involves studying demographics, such as age, gender, education level, and location, but also delving into cultural, social, and economic factors that may influence their consumer behavior. For example, if you're planning to expand into an international market, it's crucial to understand how local customs, cultural values, and traditions affect purchasing decisions. Even small details, such as your brand colors or the way you word your messaging, can have a significant impact on how they perceive your business.

In addition to knowing your consumer, it is essential to evaluate your competition. A detailed analysis of the companies already operating in the market will give you an idea of the strategies that are working, the weak points you could exploit, and the challenges you might face. Competition is not always something to be feared; it can also be a source of learning. For example, if you discover that competitors are not offering an adequate level of customer service, you could position yourself as the option that solves that need. The key is to find your differentiator, that which will make you stand out in the market.

Adapting to new markets also requires an honest assessment of your own business. Not every product or service will be a good fit for every market, and not every business has the capacity to adapt successfully. Before you take the plunge, do a thorough review of your resources, skills, and limitations. This includes assessing your production capacity, distribution channels, marketing budget, and workforce. While you may need to make adjustments in each of these areas, it's best to identify those needs early on to avoid unpleasant surprises.

One of the biggest mistakes businesses make when entering new markets is trying to replicate exactly what they've done in their original market. While it's important to maintain the essence of your brand, you also need to be willing to modify your approach as needed. For example, if your original marketing strategy relied heavily on social media, but you find that the new market relies more on word-of-mouth or traditional media, you'll need to adjust your efforts to effectively reach that audience. This level of flexibility can be the difference between success and failure.

Communication also plays an essential role in adaptation. To connect with a new market, you need to speak their language, both literally and figuratively. This means not only translating your marketing materials, but also adapting the tone, style, and messaging to resonate with your audience. Additionally, it's crucial to show cultural sensitivity. Something that may be perfectly acceptable in one market could be offensive in another. For example, certain images or phrases may have negative connotations depending on the cultural context, so it's important to test before launching any campaign.

Implementing pilot tests is another effective strategy for adapting to new markets. Instead of making a full entry right away, you can start with a limited testing phase to gauge the acceptance of your products or services. Not only will this give you valuable insights into how the market responds, but it will also reduce the financial risk associated with a full-scale expansion. Pilot tests also allow you to make adjustments before fully committing, increasing your chances of success.

Another key factor in adapting to new markets is creating strategic alliances. Working with local partners, such as distributors, retailers, or even influencers, can help you establish yourself more quickly and gain credibility in the market. These partners already understand how the local environment works and can provide you with valuable insights to help you navigate initial challenges. For example, a local distributor could help you identify the most effective sales channels, while an influencer could introduce your brand to a wider audience in an authentic way.

Adaptability also means being prepared to face unexpected challenges. Every market has its own quirks, and you're likely to face obstacles you hadn't anticipated. Maybe a competitor launches a product similar to yours just as you're entering the market, or you might find that you need to adjust your pricing model to compete. Instead of getting discouraged, view these challenges as opportunities to learn and improve. Keep an open mind and a proactive approach to problem-solving.

Finally, it's important to remember that adapting to new markets is an ongoing process. It's not enough to make an initial effort to enter the market; you also need to constantly monitor your performance, gather customer feedback, and adjust your strategy as needed. Markets change over time, and what works today might not be as effective tomorrow. The ability to evolve along with the market is what will ensure your long-term success.

Adapting to new markets is no easy task, but it is one of the most effective ways to boost your business growth. By combining thorough research, flexibility, effective communication, and careful execution, you can open up new opportunities that benefit your company and your customers. The key is to be patient, learn from the process, and be willing to make the changes necessary to succeed in an unfamiliar environment.

www.ingramcontent.com/pod-product-compliance
Lightning Source LLC
LaVergne TN
LVHW090423210926
848480LV00002B/666
* 9 7 9 8 2 3 0 0 8 9 7 1 1 *